United States Government Accountability Office

Report to Congressional Committees

July 2013

TROUBLED ASSET RELIEF PROGRAM

Treasury's Use of Auctions to Exit the Capital Purchase Program

July 2013

GAO Highlights

Highlights of GAO-13-630, a report to congressional committees

TROUBLED ASSET RELIEF PROGRAM

Treasury's Use of Auctions to Exit the Capital Purchase Program

Why GAO Did This Study

CPP was established as the primary means of restoring stability to the financial system under the Troubled Asset Relief Program (TARP). Under CPP, Treasury invested almost $205 billion in 707 eligible financial institutions between October 2008 and December 2009. As of May 31, 2013, 151 institutions remained in the program with under $6 billion in outstanding investments. TARP's authorizing legislation requires GAO to report every 60 days on TARP activities. This report examines (1) the extent to which Treasury has sold CPP investments through auctions and the returns on those investments and (2) the CPP auction process and institutions' views on the process.

To conduct its work, GAO reviewed Treasury documents and financial data on auction participants. GAO also interviewed officials from Treasury and the Securities and Exchange Commission, representatives from auction participants, and others.

View GAO-13-630. For more information, contact A. Nicole Clowers at (202) 512-8678 or clowersa@gao.gov.

What GAO Found

The U.S. Department of the Treasury (Treasury) has increasingly used auctions to sell its Capital Purchase Program (CPP) investments. Initially, Treasury relied primarily on financial institutions redeeming their shares to wind down the program. However, in March 2012 Treasury began using auctions to exit CPP, and more institutions have exited the program through auctions than through any other method since then. As of May 2013, Treasury has held 16 auctions, selling 128 investments for total proceeds of about $2.4 billion. Each auction has involved the sale of an institution's outstanding investment, also known as the par amount. In most cases, the final sales price was below the par amount, and in total Treasury received 84 percent of par in the first 16 auctions. Through these auctions, repurchases, and other mechanisms, 556 institutions had exited CPP as of May 31, 2013, accounting for almost $223 billion in repayments and income and exceeding the original investment amount by about $18 billion.

Total Sales Proceeds as a Percentage of Treasury's Outstanding Investment by Auction, as of May 31, 2013 (excludes income from repurchases, dividends, and other sources)

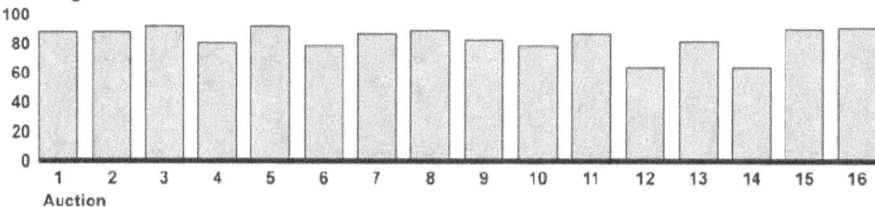

Source: GAO analysis of Treasury and SNL Financial data

Note: Auction proceeds have accounted for $2.4 billion of the nearly $223 billion in total program income. Program income to date exceeds the original investment amount by about $18 billion.

Treasury has structured the auctions to maximize taxpayer returns, but representatives from some of the 13 financial institutions that participated in the auctions told GAO that they had concerns about the process. Treasury selected institutions for auctions based on, among other things, the size of the institution's CPP investment and its dividend payment record. Treasury then notified the institutions that their securities were going to be auctioned, and the institutions were required to submit certain documentation to Treasury. Representatives of some institutions, mostly from earlier auctions, told GAO that the process was rushed and left them with limited notice to prepare the required documentation and insufficient time to obtain regulatory approval to bid on their own shares. Treasury officials said they would have been willing to move an institution to a later auction if it needed more time to prepare, and while representatives of a few institutions that participated in later auctions felt the process was rushed, other institutions said they had more time to prepare. Representatives of some institutions expressed frustration that they did not have the option to match the winning bid to retain ownership of their shares. Treasury officials said that any changes to the process that benefitted the financial institution would make the process less competitive for other bidders at the expense of taxpayers and would contradict Treasury's goal of structuring the process to increase competition and maximize returns for taxpayers.

_____ **United States Government Accountability Office**

Contents

GAO
441 G St. N.W.
Washington, DC 20548

U.S. GOVERNMENT ACCOUNTABILITY OFFICE

July 8, 2013

Congressional Committees

The Capital Purchase Program (CPP), the first and largest initiative under the Troubled Asset Relief Program (TARP), provided almost $205 billion in capital to eligible financial institutions by purchasing preferred shares and subordinated debt.[1] In return for its investments, the U.S. Department of the Treasury (Treasury) received dividend or interest payments and warrants.[2] The program was closed to new investments on December 31, 2009, and since then Treasury has continued to oversee and divest its CPP investments, collect dividend and interest payments, and sell warrants. Recently Treasury has taken steps to wind down this bank investment program with a focus on auctioning the participating financial institutions' preferred shares.

Under our statutorily mandated responsibilities for providing timely oversight of TARP, we have been monitoring and providing updates on TARP programs, including CPP.[3] This report examines (1) the extent to which Treasury had sold CPP investments through auctions and the

---

[1]As authorized by the Emergency Economic Stabilization Act of 2008 (EESA), Pub. L. No. 110-343, 122 Stat. 3765 (2008), codified at 12 U.S.C. §§ 5201 et seq. EESA, which was signed into law on October 3, 2008, established the Office of Financial Stability within the Department of the Treasury and provided it with broad, flexible authorities to buy or guarantee troubled mortgage-related assets or any other financial instruments necessary to stabilize the financial markets.

[2]A warrant is an option to buy shares of common stock or preferred stock at a predetermined price on or before a specified date.

[3]We must report at least every 60 days on findings resulting from oversight of TARP's performance in meeting the purposes of EESA, the financial condition and internal controls of TARP, the characteristics of both asset purchases and the disposition of assets acquired, TARP's efficiency in using the funds appropriated for the program's operation, TARP's compliance with applicable laws and regulations, and other matters. 12 U.S.C. § 5226(a). See, for example, GAO, *Capital Purchase Program: Status of the Program and Financial Health of Remaining Participants*, GAO-13-458 (Washington, D.C.: May 7, 2013), *Capital Purchase Program: Revenues Have Exceeded Investments, but Concerns about Outstanding Investments Remain*, GAO-12-301 (Washington, D.C.: Mar. 8, 2012), and *Troubled Asset Relief Program: Opportunities Exist to Apply Lessons Learned from the Capital Purchase Program to Similarly Designed Programs and to Improve the Repayment Process*, GAO-11-47 (Washington, D.C.: Oct. 4, 2010).

GAO-13-630 Troubled Asset Relief Program

returns on those investments and (2) the CPP auction process and institutions' views on the process.

To examine the extent to which Treasury has sold CPP investments through auctions and the returns on those investments, we collected data from Treasury and SNL Financial on the results of recent auctions, including the names of participating institutions, sale prices for the shares auctioned by Treasury, and the dollar amount of the shares sold below par value. We assessed the reliability of the Treasury and SNL Financial data and determined that they were sufficiently reliable to describe the results of CPP auctions. To review the CPP auction process, we reviewed relevant Treasury documents and interviewed Treasury officials, individuals knowledgeable about auctions of CPP investments, representatives of institutions that participated in the auction process. trade associations representing financial institutions, and officials from the Securities and Exchange Commission (SEC). We selected participating institutions to interview based on when the institutions went to auction, geographic diversity, and a sample of both private and public institutions. Appendix I contains additional information on our scope and methodology.

We conducted this performance audit from January 2013 to July 2013 in accordance with generally accepted government auditing standards. Those standards require that we plan and perform the audit to obtain sufficient, appropriate evidence to provide a reasonable basis for our findings and conclusions based on our audit objectives. We believe that the evidence obtained provides a reasonable basis for our findings and conclusions based on our audit objectives.

Background

Created in 2008, CPP was the primary initiative under TARP to help stabilize the financial markets and banking system by providing capital to qualifying regulated financial institutions through the purchase of senior preferred shares and subordinated debt.[4] Instead of purchasing troubled mortgage-backed securities and whole loans, as initially envisioned under TARP, Treasury used CPP investments to strengthen financial institutions' capital levels. Treasury determined that strengthening capital

---

[4]For purposes of CPP, qualifying financial institutions generally include stand-alone U.S.-controlled banks and savings associations, as well as bank holding companies and most savings and loan holding companies.

levels was the more effective mechanism to help stabilize financial markets, encourage interbank lending, and increase confidence in lenders and investors. Treasury anticipated that strengthening the capital positions of the financial institutions would enhance confidence in the institutions themselves and the financial system overall and increase the institutions' capacity to undertake new lending and support the economy. On October 14, 2008, Treasury allocated $250 billion of the original $700 billion in overall TARP funds for CPP. The allocation was subsequently reduced in March 2009 to reflect lower estimated funding needs, as evidenced by actual participation rates. The program was closed to new investments on December 31, 2009. The Office of Financial Stability was established within Treasury to implement TARP in consultation with federal banking regulators.

Under CPP, qualified financial institutions were eligible to receive an investment of between 1 and 3 percent of their risk-weighted assets, up to a maximum of $25 billion.[5] In exchange for the investment, Treasury generally received senior preferred shares that would pay dividends at a rate of 5 percent annually for the first 5 years and 9 percent annually thereafter.[6] Treasury was also required to receive warrants to purchase shares of common or preferred stock or a senior debt instrument to further protect taxpayers and help ensure returns on the investments. Institutions are allowed to repay CPP investments with the approval of their primary federal bank regulator and afterward to redeem warrants.

Nine major financial institutions were initially included in CPP because Treasury and the federal banking regulators considered them essential to

---

[5]Risk-weighted assets are all assets and off-balance-sheet items held by an institution, weighted for risk according to the federal banking agencies' regulatory capital standards. In May 2009, Treasury increased the maximum amount of CPP funding that small financial institutions (qualifying financial institutions with total assets of less than $500 million) could receive from 3 to 5 percent of risk-weighted assets.

[6]Some other types of institutions, such as S corporations, received their CPP investment in the form of subordinated debt and pay Treasury interest rather than dividends Treasury received subordinated debt rather than preferred shares in order to preserve these institutions' special tax status. The U.S. Internal Revenue Code prohibits S corporations from having more than one class of stock outstanding. Interest rates for this debt are 7.7 percent for the first 5 years and 13.8 percent for the remaining years.

the operation of the financial system.[7] At the time, these nine institutions held about 55 percent of U.S. banking assets and provided a variety of services, including retail, wholesale, and investment banking and custodial and processing services. According to Treasury officials, the nine financial institutions agreed to participate in CPP in part to signal the program's importance to the stability of the financial system. Initially, Treasury approved $125 billion in total capital purchases for these institutions and completed the transactions with eight of them on October 28, 2008, for a total of $115 billion. The remaining $10 billion was disbursed after the merger of Bank of America Corporation and Merrill Lynch & Co., Inc. was completed in January 2009. Treasury ultimately disbursed about $205 billion to 707 financial institutions through December 2009. Participating institutions began repaying their investments and exiting CPP in early 2009.

In May 2012, Treasury announced a strategy to wind down its remaining investments. Treasury's strategy includes three options that, according to Treasury officials, aim to protect taxpayer interests, promote financial stability, and preserve the strength of the nation's community banks. Treasury's options include (1) repayments, (2) restructurings, and (3) auctions. According to Treasury officials, Treasury conducts analyses to determine which option is most appropriate for a particular institution.

- Repayments allow financial institutions, with the approval of their regulators, to redeem their preferred shares in full. Treasury noted that institutions have the legal right to do this at any time. A majority of institutions have exited the program in this manner since 2009, and Treasury expected some financial institutions to continue to use it through late 2013. Under this option, Treasury's ability to exit the program largely depends on the ability of institutions to repay their investments. In particular, institutions must demonstrate that they are financially strong enough to repay the CPP investments in order to receive regulatory approval to exit the program. Dividend rates will increase from 5 percent to 9 percent for remaining institutions beginning in late 2013, a development that may prompt institutions to repay their investments. If broader interest rates are low, especially

---

[7]The nine major financial institutions were Bank of America Corporation; Citigroup, Inc.; JPMorgan Chase & Co.; Wells Fargo & Company; Morgan Stanley; The Goldman Sachs Group, Inc.; The Bank of New York Mellon Corporation; State Street Corporation; and Merrill Lynch & Co., Inc.

GAO-13-630 Troubled Asset Relief Program

approaching the dividend reset, the financial institutions could have further incentive to redeem their preferred shares. Treasury intends to continue using the repayment option for institutions that it believes are capable of redeeming all shares in full in the near future, but Treasury officials said that the number of such institutions was declining.

- Restructurings allow troubled financial institutions to restructure their investments, and all restructurings require new capital —for example, from a merger. With this option, Treasury receives cash or other securities that generally can be sold more easily than preferred stock, but Treasury's investments are sometimes sold at a discount. As such, Treasury has used restructurings as a means of winding down CPP investments only on a limited basis. Although Treasury officials expect a limited number of restructurings to continue, they told us that they would approve the sales only if the terms represented the best deal for taxpayers.

- Auctions allow Treasury to sell its preferred stock. Treasury conducted the first auction of CPP investments in March 2012 and reported that it generated strong investor interest. Treasury also reported that this option could be beneficial for community banks that did not have easy access to the capital markets, because it could attract new, private capital to replace the temporary TARP support. Treasury expects this option to continue to be part of its effort to wind down CPP. Thus far, Treasury has sold investments individually but noted that it might combine other investments, particularly smaller investments, into pooled auctions. Unlike Treasury's recent auctions of individual CPP preferred stock investments, in which multiple bidders were allocated portions of the preferred stock at a single clearing price, Treasury anticipates that the pooled auctions will result in a single highest bidder purchasing all of the securities included in the pool. Whether Treasury sells stock individually or in pools, the outcome of this option will depend largely on investor demand for these securities.

In considering these options, we have previously noted that Treasury will need to balance the goals of protecting taxpayer-supported investments while expeditiously unwinding the program.[8] Treasury officials said that

---

[8]See GAO, *Troubled Asset Relief Program: Treasury Sees Some Returns as It Exits Programs and Continues to Fund Mortgage Programs*, GAO-13-192 (Washington, D.C.: Jan. 7, 2013).

they would continue to evaluate the CPP exit strategy but added that they expected to continue using these options for the foreseeable future.

As of May 31, 2013, Treasury had received $222.6 billion in repayments and income, exceeding the $204.9 billion originally disbursed by almost $18 billion (see fig. 1).[9] Further, 556 institutions had exited CPP as of May 31, 2013, including 212 institutions that exited by fully repaying their CPP investments, 128 that participated in auctions, and 165 that refinanced their investments through other federal programs.[10] The $222.6 billion in total proceeds includes $193.5 billion in repayments; $2.4 billion in auction sales of original CPP investments; $18.9 billion in dividends, interest, and other income; and $7.9 billion in warrants sold. After accounting for write-offs and realized losses totaling $3.4 billion, CPP had $5.6 billion in outstanding investments as of May 31, 2013.

Figure 1: Status of Capital Purchase Program Funds and Participants, as of May 31, 2013

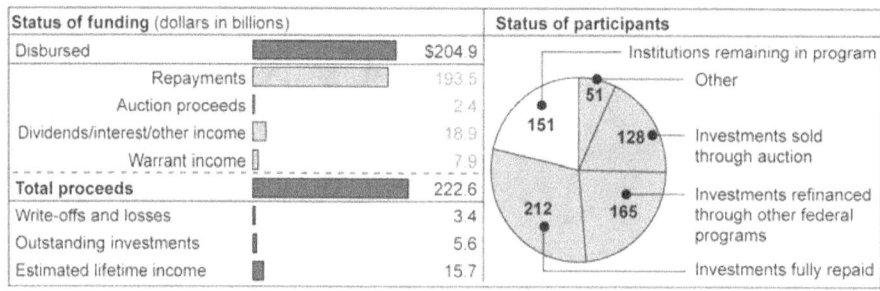

Source: GAO analysis of Treasury data

Note: Treasury estimates its lifetime income on a quarterly basis using the aggregate value of investments at market prices in conjunction with the Office of Management and Budget and publishes them in its monthly reports to Congress. The amount of estimated lifetime income is as of March 31, 2013.

---

[9]Treasury, *Troubled Asset Relief Program (TARP) Monthly Report to Congress – May 2013* (June 10, 2013).

[10]Of the 165 institutions, 28 exited through the Community Development Capital Initiative, and 137 exited through the Small Business Lending Fund. Additionally, 25 institutions went into bankruptcy or receivership, 22 had their investments sold by Treasury, and 4 merged with another institution. Further, 11 institutions have made partial repayments but remain in the program.

GAO-13-630 Troubled Asset Relief Program

Treasury Has Increasingly Used Auctions to Wind Down CPP

Treasury has increasingly used the auction option after the first sale of CPP securities in March 2012 received investor interest. Through February 2012, 148 institutions had exited CPP by redeeming their preferred shares in full. As figure 2 shows, from March 2012—the month of Treasury's first auction—through May 2013, 64 institutions exited by redeeming their investments while 128 institutions exited through 16 auctions.[11]

Figure 2: Institutions Exiting the Capital Purchase Program by Repayments and Auctions, from February 2010 to May 2013

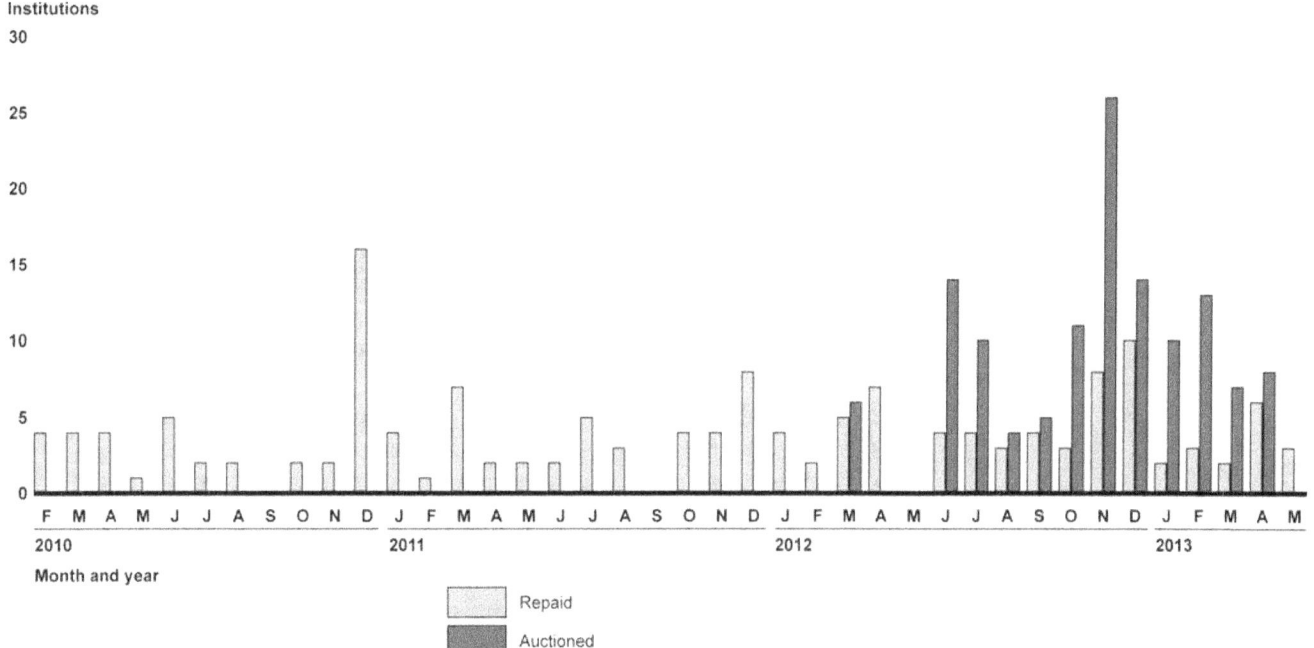

Source: GAO analysis of Treasury and SNL Financial data

Note: CPP participants began repaying their investments in early 2009, and as of January 31, 2010, 58 participants had made full repayments.

Each auction involved the sale of an institution's outstanding CPP investment, also known as the par amount. In most cases, the final sales price for an institution's shares was below the par amount. In particular,

---

[11]Treasury conducted its 17th auction in June 2013, resulting in the sale of investments in six institutions. We did not include this auction in our analysis because it occurred after we had concluded our audit work.

GAO-13-630 Troubled Asset Relief Program

the $2.4 billion in total proceeds from the 16 auctions to date—from March 2012 through April 2013— represents 84 percent of the $2.9 billion principal investment in the institutions.[12] For each round of auctions, the percentage of par amount that Treasury received ranged from 65 percent in the 12th auction to 93 percent in the 5th auction (see fig. 3). Out of all institutions that participated in these 16 auctions, final sales prices for individual institutions ranged from 17 percent to 131 percent of par. Treasury officials said that the auction results reflected the potential risk associated with the liquidity of the investment and the credit quality of the financial institutions, including their ability to make future dividend or interest payments, as well as the prospect of receiving previous missed payments that had accrued. For example, later auctions tended to include smaller institutions with more cumulative missed payments. In a few cases, the prospect of recouping these missed payments made them particularly attractive to investors and helped a number of institutions to sell shares at above their par value. Although Treasury has not generally recouped its full investment in individual institutions through the auctions, Treasury officials told us that accepting a discount and transferring ownership of these institutions to the private sector was in the best interest of the taxpayer. Because of the inherent risk factors of these institutions, Treasury officials did not believe that these institutions would be able to make full repayments in the near future. The officials added that had they chosen not to auction these positions, their values could have decreased later. Treasury officials also said that while auctions were generally priced at a discount to par, the prices were generally equal to or above Treasury's internal valuations.

---

[12]According to Treasury officials, Treasury's total receipts from the 128 financial institutions that exited CPP through auctions—which includes auction proceeds as well as warrant proceeds and dividends—is slightly greater than Treasury's $2.9 billion principal investment in these institutions.

GAO-13-630 Troubled Asset Relief Program

Figure 3: Total Sales Proceeds as a Percentage of Treasury's Outstanding Investment (Par Amount) by Auction, as of May 31, 2013

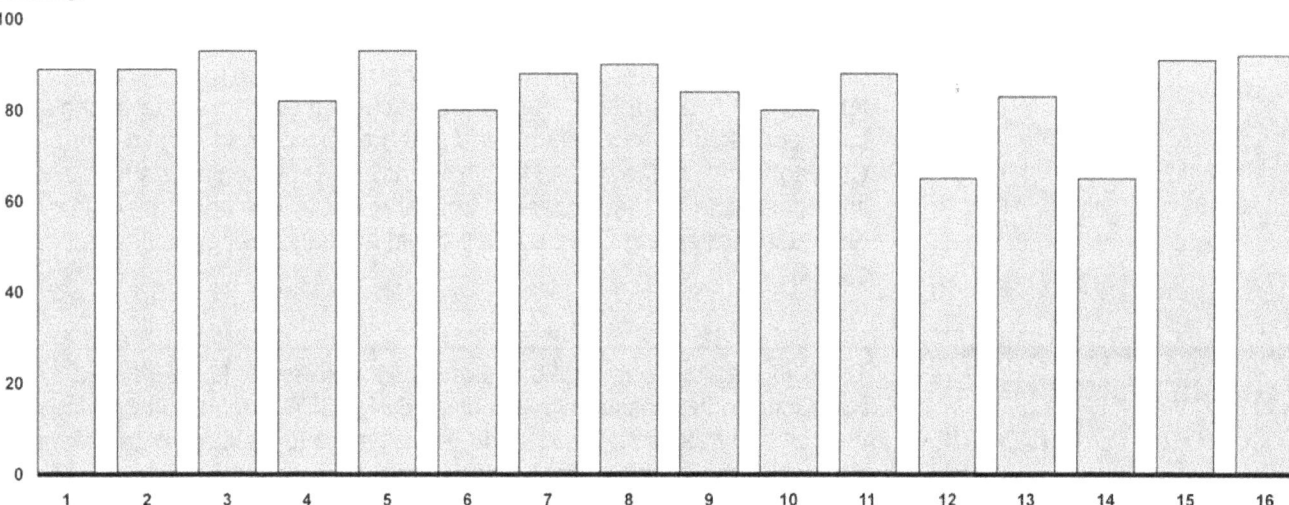

Source: GAO analysis of Treasury and SNL Financial data.

Note: Each round of auctions included multiple institutions whose assets were sold separately, and the bars represent total proceeds from all institutions in each round of auctions. For individual institutions, final sales prices ranged from 17 percent to 131 percent of par.

According to representatives from some financial institutions that participated in the auctions, there are many reasons for seeking to exit CPP, including through the auction process. In particular, representatives from several institutions told us that compensation restrictions provided a strong incentive to exit. That is, as a condition of receiving TARP assistance, the financial institutions must meet a number of requirements related to incentive and bonus compensation arrangements for senior executive officers. Representatives from other institutions told us that there was a stigma associated with remaining in the program. As we have reported, Treasury officials said that the public's negative opinion of TARP curtailed overall interest and participation in the program.[13] Representatives from some institutions also said that the impending

---

[13]See GAO, *Troubled Asset Relief Program: Status of Programs and Implementation of GAO Recommendations*, GAO-11-74 (Washington, D.C.: Jan. 12, 2011).

GAO-13-630 Troubled Asset Relief Program

increase in the dividend rate from 5 percent to 9 percent provided a strong incentive to redeem the shares if the institution was able to do so.

Treasury has stated that the auction process could be beneficial for financial institutions that do not have easy access to the capital markets, because the auctions could attract new private capital to replace the temporary TARP support. Further, representatives from some financial institutions told us that they agreed that the auction had helped them exit CPP sooner than they could have otherwise. Representatives from other institutions told us that access to capital markets was not a major factor in their plans for exiting CPP, as they could have independently raised the capital.

Treasury Structured Auctions to Maximize Taxpayer Return, but Some Auction Participants Have Raised Concerns about the Process

Treasury began planning its auctions in November 2011 by hiring a contractor to help assess its exit strategy for CPP. Among other things, the company assisted Treasury in reaching out to institutions to determine if they had the intent and ability to redeem their preferred shares in the near future. For those institutions that would not be redeeming in the near future, Treasury, with the company's assistance, later contacted them to discuss the auction process. Treasury held the first "pilot" auction in March 2012 to determine investor interest in CPP securities. Of the remaining institutions, Treasury said that it selected for this auction the preferred stocks of six financial institutions that had existing effective shelf registration statements and whose assets could thus be auctioned most quickly.[14] Treasury officials said that they focused on the shares of those institutions in order to test the efficacy of the auction process.

In May 2012, Treasury outlined its strategy for winding down CPP, citing the auction option as one that would help a number of institutions exit the program. Treasury, with assistance from its contractor, began by assessing the financial institutions that remained in CPP to determine their suitability for individual auctions. Treasury officials said that it used a number of criteria to make this determination including the size of the institution's CPP investment, the existence of an effective shelf

---

[14]A shelf registration, under SEC Rule 415, exists when, in certain situations, a corporation can file a registration statement and wait up to 3 years until the public offering takes place, as long as it has filed all required reports in a timely manner.

registration, and the institution's record of paying its dividends.[15] For the initial auctions, Treasury selected larger, publicly traded institutions that were up to date on their dividend payments. For example, 17 of the 20 institutions participating in the first three auctions had over $1 billion in assets. Furthermore, four of the first five auctions included only publicly held institutions.

After selecting the institutions, Treasury notified them that they would be part of an upcoming auction, and the institutions then had to assemble and submit documentation to Treasury. Documentation requirements were based on the nature of the offering. For example, publicly traded institutions selected for auctions had to submit a prospectus supplement and an underwriting agreement. Further, privately held institutions had to submit a placement agency agreement that included a number of disclosures relating to capital levels and dividend payment history. If an institution wanted to bid on its own shares in the auction it also needed to get approval from its primary federal regulator. In the days before the auction, Treasury notified potential investors by issuing a press release of the institutions that were to be auctioned. Treasury used a modified Dutch auction process, which established a market price by allowing investors to submit bids at specified increments above a minimum price that was specified for each auction.[16] After the auctions closed, Treasury published the results in press releases.

In the 16 auctions to date, Treasury sold multiple, individual CPP investments at each auction. In particular, multiple bidders were allocated portions of the preferred stock at a single clearing price for each institution. However, in June 2012 Treasury notified about 200 financial institutions that it was considering including them as part of a series of pooled auctions that were to begin in the fall of 2012. Treasury began

---

[15]Dividend or interest payments are due on a quarterly basis, but institutions can elect whether to pay dividends and may choose not to pay for a variety of reasons. For example, the institution or its federal and state regulators may decide not to pay dividends to conserve cash and maintain (or increase) capital levels. However, unpaid cumulative dividends generally accrue and the institution must pay them before making payments to other types of shareholders, such as holders of common stock.

[16]A Dutch auction is a method for pricing shares whereby the price of the shares offered is lowered until there are enough bids to sell all the shares. All shares are sold at that price. Modified Dutch auctions usually have a certain lower limit that the auctioneer cannot go below and are used mainly when a quick sale is required. Treasury had previously used Dutch auctions to sell its CPP warrants.

considering pooled auctions for the positions—which were smaller than the previously auctioned positions—out of concern that Treasury might not be able to generate sufficient interest in these positions individually to conduct a competitive auction. Treasury anticipates that pooled auctions will result in a single highest bidder purchasing all of the securities of all institutions included in the pool. Treasury offered these financial institutions the opportunity to opt out of the pooled auction by submitting an "opt-out" bid to repurchase all of their outstanding CPP securities. Treasury also provided these institutions with the option of arranging for a designated bidder to repurchase their shares at auction, giving the institutions an additional opportunity to avoid the possibility of gaining new unfamiliar shareholders.[17]

If the institution's or its designated bidder's bid met a minimum price level set by Treasury, Treasury would remove the institution from the potential pooled auction and schedule it for an individual auction or other sale later. However, Treasury advised the institutions that a decision to remove them from a pooled auction did not mean that the institutions, or their designated bidders, were entitled to purchase the investment at the submitted bid price. Further, Treasury told institutions that it would determine at a later date whether to conduct an individual auction or use another mechanism to recoup its investments. Treasury originally set the deadline for submitting the opt-out bid in August 2012. However, after receiving feedback that some institutions needed more time to obtain approval from their regulators, it extended the deadline to October 2012 and later extended it again to April 2013. Treasury began including institutions that had opted out of a potential pooled auction in the seventh auction, which occurred in October 2012. As of June 2013, Treasury had not scheduled any pooled auctions.

---

[17]As part of the pooled auction process, Treasury gave the financial institutions the option of designating a single outside investor, or single group of investors, to make a bid to purchase all the institution's outstanding CPP securities. Similar to bidding on its own shares, an institution using a designated bidder had to obtain approval from its primary federal regulator.

Representatives from financial institutions with whom we spoke had varied experiences with the auction process and some cited a number of concerns with the process, including the following.[18]

- **Timing and organization of the process.** Representatives from many of the 13 financial institutions with whom we spoke—particularly those that had participated in some of the earlier auctions—thought that the process of preparing for the auction was rushed, was not well organized, and did not have clear instructions. In particular, representatives from multiple institutions that we interviewed said that they had about 3 weeks from the time they were contacted by Treasury to prepare and submit documentation for the auction. According to some of these representatives, this amount of time was not sufficient to get regulatory approval to bid on their own shares. Representatives from many of the institutions that we interviewed also told us that the process was frustrating because Treasury did not provide clear guidance for preparing documentation and disclosures, causing them to incur significant expenses—cited as ranging from $50,000 to $300,000 among the institutions we interviewed—to hire lawyers and accountants to prepare documentation. In contrast, while representatives from a few institutions that participated in later auctions felt the process was rushed, others told us that they had much more time to prepare for their auctions—up to 10 months in some cases.

  Treasury officials told us that they began reaching out to potential auction participants in July 2011 to determine their plans for exiting CPP and discuss the potential auctions. Although Treasury did not begin discussing specific documentation requirements until it notified a financial institution that it was scheduled for a particular upcoming auction, Treasury officials said that they would have been willing to move an institution that need more time to prepare to a later. Finally, Treasury officials said that they would not expect the auction process to be consistent for all auction participants, as a number of factors could affect the amount of time an institution needed to prepare for an auction. For example, institutions wishing to bid on their own shares at

---

[18]While we selected a diverse group of auction participants to interview, their statements reflect their specific experiences and should not be generalized to reflect the views of all auction participants.

auction would require additional time to obtain regulatory approval compared to institutions that did not plan to submit their own bids.

- **Use of opt-out bid.** Representatives from some institutions we interviewed expressed frustration that Treasury used the institution's opt-out bid as the minimum bid for the auctions. According to representatives from many of the financial institutions with whom we spoke that had opted out of the pooled auction process, they were surprised that their opt-out bid was used as the floor price in the auction process. These representatives said that Treasury did not tell them that their opt-out bid would be used as a floor price and that they only found out when the auction began. Representatives from one institution told us that Treasury did not notify them of this practice but that they discovered it from other institutions that had already gone to auction. Many of the representatives said they would have submitted a higher bid in order to win the auction and retain ownership if they had known that the opt-out bid would be used this way.

  According to Treasury officials, financial institutions selected for the pooled auctions would generally have a more difficult time being sold individually at an auction, and the purpose of the minimum price, which Treasury sets, is to ensure that any bids submitted at auction would be at prices acceptable to Treasury. Treasury officials noted that the opt-out bid may be the minimum price for an auction, and that Treasury retains full discretion to determine what the minimum price should be. The officials also said that the minimum price was disclosed at the beginning of each auction and that Treasury notified institutions that intended to bid on their own shares prior to the auction so that the institution can finalize disclosure documents. Treasury officials said that in the event that the clearing price was equal to the opt-out price, the institution (or its designated bidder, if applicable) would win all of its shares. Treasury officials also said that all institutions had the option at auction to submit a bid above the minimum price and that many institutions had done so. Finally, Treasury officials said that any changes to the process that benefit the financial institution would make the process less competitive for other bidders at the expense of taxpayers.

- **Disclosure requirement.** Representatives from some publicly traded financial institutions with whom we spoke expressed frustration over SEC's requirement that they publicly disclose their intent to bid on their own shares and the amount of capital they raised to do so. Representatives from these institutions—which had internal, nonpublic information available to them—said that this disclosure requirement signaled to other bidders that the shares were an attractive investment, raising the prices. Some financial institution representatives also felt that they were at a disadvantage because the other bidders knew, through the disclosure required by SEC, the amount of capital the participant had available for bidding on its shares. Conversely, the financial institutions had no knowledge about the capital available to the other potential bidders. While the disclosures may have resulted in higher returns to Treasury, representatives from some of these institutions said the disclosures put them at a disadvantage compared to the other bidders. According to SEC officials, the purpose of the disclosure was to protect investors by alerting them to the fact that the clearing price for the securities offered in the auction could be affected by the institution's bids. The officials also said that this information was particularly relevant because even assuming the institution has disclosed all material, non-public information to investors, the institution is always better informed about its performance and prospects than any bidder or other third party.

- **No matching bids.** A number of financial institutions told us that they would have preferred the option of matching the winning bid to be able to retain ownership of their shares. However, Treasury officials said that changes to the process benefitting the financial institutions would make the process less competitive to potential bidders and less beneficial for the taxpayer. In particular, Treasury officials said that giving the institution the right to match the winning bid would make other bidders less competitive, and could, in turn, discourage potential bidders from participating.

Some of the concerns with the auction process cited by auction participants with whom we spoke may have been caused by a difference in motivations. According to a banking association, banks generally like to retain ownership. Treasury officials said that their goal was to create a competitive and transparent process that would maximize returns to taxpayers. Treasury said that the auctions had been successful in helping Treasury to wind down CPP and transfer ownership of the preferred shares to the private sector.

Agency Comments and Our Evaluation

We provided a draft of this report to Treasury for its review and comment. Treasury provided written comments that we have reprinted in appendix II. In its written comments, Treasury noted that the report provided a helpful overview of its strategy to wind down CPP. It also noted that

Treasury had realized a positive return of $17.8 billion on its CPP investments as of June 28, 2013, and that 143 institutions remained in the program representing a remaining investment of $5.5 billion. Treasury also emphasized TARP's effectiveness in preventing a collapse of the financial system and in restarting economic growth.

We are sending copies of this report to the Financial Stability Oversight Board, the Special Inspector General for TARP, interested congressional committees and members, and Treasury. The report also is available at no charge on the GAO website at http://www.gao.gov.

If you or your staffs have any questions about this report, please contact A. Nicole Clowers at (202) 512-8678 or clowersa@gao.gov. Contact points for our Offices of Congressional Relations and Public Affairs may be found on the last page of this report. GAO staff who made major contributions to this report are listed in appendix III.

A. Nicole Clowers
Director
Financial Markets and Community Investment

List of Addressees

The Honorable Barbara Mikulski
Chairwoman
The Honorable Richard C. Shelby
Vice Chairman
Committee on Appropriations
United States Senate

The Honorable Tim Johnson
Chairman
The Honorable Mike Crapo
Ranking Member
Committee on Banking, Housing, and Urban Affairs
United States Senate

The Honorable Patty Murray
Chairman
The Honorable Jeff Sessions
Ranking Member
Committee on the Budget
United States Senate

The Honorable Max Baucus
Chairman
The Honorable Orrin G. Hatch
Ranking Member
Committee on Finance
United States Senate

The Honorable Hal Rogers
Chairman
The Honorable Nita Lowey
Ranking Member
Committee on Appropriations
House of Representatives

The Honorable Paul Ryan
Chairman
The Honorable Chris Van Hollen
Ranking Member
Committee on the Budget
House of Representatives

The Honorable Jeb Hensarling
Chairman
The Honorable Maxine Waters
Ranking Member
Committee on Financial Services
House of Representatives

The Honorable Dave Camp
Chairman
The Honorable Sander Levin
Ranking Member
Committee on Ways and Means
House of Representatives

Appendix I: Objectives, Scope, and Methodology

The objectives of our report were to assess (1) the extent to which Treasury had sold Capital Purchase Program (CPP) investments through auctions and the returns on those investments; and (2) the CPP auction process and institutions' views on the process. To assess Treasury's wind-down strategy for CPP, we reviewed Treasury press releases and interviewed Treasury officials on their auction implementation strategy. To analyze the auction results, we reviewed data from Treasury and SNL Financial—a private company that maintains a database of information from publicly filed regulatory and financial reports—on the results of recent auctions. The data included information on the names of participating institutions, the par value of shares sold at auction, and the sale prices for the shares, among other things. To obtain institutions' views on the process, we interviewed representatives of 13 institutions that had participated in the auction process. In selecting participating institutions to interview, we sought representation from participants in early as well as more recent auctions, geographic diversity, and a balance of both private and public institutions. While we selected a diverse group of auction participants to interview, their statements reflect their specific experiences and should not be generalized to reflect the views of all auction participants. We also interviewed individuals knowledgeable about the CPP auction process, representatives from trade associations for financial institutions, and officials from the Securities and Exchange Commission.

We determined that the CPP program data from Treasury were sufficiently reliable to assess the status of the program and the results of CPP auctions. For example, we tested the Office of Financial Stability's internal controls over financial reporting as they related to our annual audit of the office's financial statements and found the information to be sufficiently reliable based on the results of our audits of fiscal years 2009, 2010, 2011, and 2012 financial statements for TARP.[1] We also compared Treasury's auction data to comparable data from SNL Financial and

---

[1] See GAO, *Financial Audit: Office of Financial Stability (Troubled Asset Relief Program) Fiscal Years 2012 and 2011 Financial Statements*, GAO-13-126R (Washington, D.C.: Nov. 9, 2012); *Financial Audit: Office of Financial Stability (Troubled Asset Relief Program) Fiscal Years 2011 and 2010 Financial Statements*, GAO-12-169 (Washington, D.C.: Nov.10, 2011); *Financial Audit: Office of Financial Stability (Troubled Asset Relief Program) Fiscal Years 2010 and 2009 Financial Statements*, GAO-11-174 (Washington, D.C.: Nov.15, 2010); and *Financial Audit: Office of Financial Stability (Troubled Asset Relief Program) Fiscal Year 2009 Financial Statements*, GAO-10-301 (Washington, D.C.: Dec. 9, 2009).

accounted for any differences. We assessed the reliability of SNL
Financial data as part of previous studies and found the data to be
reliable for the purposes of our review. We verified that no changes had
been made that would affect the data's reliability.

We conducted this performance audit from January 2013 to July 2013 in
accordance with generally accepted government auditing standards.
Those standards require that we plan and perform the audit to obtain
sufficient, appropriate evidence to provide a reasonable basis for our
findings and conclusions based on our audit objectives. We believe that
the evidence obtained provides a reasonable basis for our findings and
conclusions based on our audit objectives.

Appendix II: Comments from the Office of Financial Stability

DEPARTMENT OF THE TREASURY
WASHINGTON, D.C.

June 28, 2013

ASSISTANT SECRETARY

A. Nicole Clowers
Director
Financial Markets and Community Investment
U.S. Government Accountability Office
441 G Street, NW
Washington, DC 20548

Dear Ms. Clowers:

I am writing in response to your draft report regarding the Capital Purchase Program (CPP), entitled, *Troubled Asset Relief Program: Treasury's Use of Auctions to Exit the Capital Purchase Program* (Draft Report). The Department of the Treasury (Treasury) appreciates the efforts of the Government Accountability Office (GAO), and this letter provides our official comments to the Draft Report.

The Draft Report provides a helpful overview of Treasury's three-pronged strategy to wind down CPP, which involves: (1) waiting for repayments from those banks who can repay the TARP investment in full in the near future, (2) selling through competitive auctions investments in banks that cannot repay in the near future, and (3) restructuring some investments, typically in connection with a merger or infusion of new capital, if the same represents the best option for the taxpayer. As of today, Treasury has recovered $222.7 billion on an initial CPP investment of $204.9 billion – representing a gain of $17.8 billion. Only 143 of the 707 original CPP participants are still in the program, representing a remaining Treasury investment of only $5.5 billion.

The recovery for CPP is similar to the situation with respect to all the TARP bank programs as well as TARP as a whole. For all TARP programs, we have collected $400 billion against disbursements of $420 billion. And, for the TARP investment programs as a whole—that is, excluding disbursements for housing, which were never meant to be recovered, and including all investments made in banks, the auto industry, the credit markets, and AIG—Treasury invested a total of $412 billion and has collected over $417 billion, if one includes the proceeds of all Treasury's shares in AIG.

While it is good news that we are continuing to wind-down the investment programs quickly and, in almost all cases, at a gain to the taxpayer, the most important measure of success is that these programs were effective in helping to prevent the collapse of the financial system and in restarting economic growth. While there is still more work to be done, it is clear that the damage to our economy would have been far worse, and the costs far greater without the government's forceful response. And, to mitigate the risks in the future, we are putting in place a comprehensive set of reforms to make the financial system safer and stronger.

Treasury values GAO's review of the CPP wind down process and looks forward to continuing to work with you and your team as we move forward.

Sincerely,

Timothy G. Massad
Assistant Secretary for Financial Stability

Appendix III: GAO Contact and Staff Acknowledgments

GAO Contact	A. Nicole Clowers, (202) 512-8678 or clowersa@gao.gov
Staff Acknowledgments	In addition to the contact named above, Karen Tremba (Assistant Director), Christopher Forys, Michael Mikota, Emily Chalmers, William Chatlos, Marc Molino, and Patricia Moye made significant contributions to this report.

GAO's Mission	The Government Accountability Office, the audit, evaluation, and investigative arm of Congress, exists to support Congress in meeting its constitutional responsibilities and to help improve the performance and accountability of the federal government for the American people. GAO examines the use of public funds; evaluates federal programs and policies; and provides analyses, recommendations, and other assistance to help Congress make informed oversight, policy, and funding decisions. GAO's commitment to good government is reflected in its core values of accountability, integrity, and reliability.
Obtaining Copies of GAO Reports and Testimony	The fastest and easiest way to obtain copies of GAO documents at no cost is through GAO's website (http://www.gao.gov). Each weekday afternoon, GAO posts on its website newly released reports, testimony, and correspondence. To have GAO e-mail you a list of newly posted products, go to http://www.gao.gov and select "E-mail Updates."
Order by Phone	The price of each GAO publication reflects GAO's actual cost of production and distribution and depends on the number of pages in the publication and whether the publication is printed in color or black and white. Pricing and ordering information is posted on GAO's website, http://www.gao.gov/ordering.htm. Place orders by calling (202) 512-6000, toll free (866) 801-7077, or TDD (202) 512-2537. Orders may be paid for using American Express, Discover Card, MasterCard, Visa, check, or money order. Call for additional information.
Connect with GAO	Connect with GAO on Facebook, Flickr, Twitter, and YouTube. Subscribe to our RSS Feeds or E-mail Updates. Listen to our Podcasts. Visit GAO on the web at www.gao.gov.
To Report Fraud, Waste, and Abuse in Federal Programs	Contact: Website: http://www.gao.gov/fraudnet/fraudnet.htm E-mail: fraudnet@gao.gov Automated answering system: (800) 424-5454 or (202) 512-7470
Congressional Relations	Katherine Siggerud, Managing Director, siggerudk@gao.gov, (202) 512-4400, U.S. Government Accountability Office, 441 G Street NW, Room 7125, Washington, DC 20548
Public Affairs	Chuck Young, Managing Director, youngc1@gao.gov, (202) 512-4800 U.S. Government Accountability Office, 441 G Street NW, Room 7149 Washington, DC 20548

www.ingramcontent.com/pod-product-compliance
Lightning Source LLC
Chambersburg PA
CBHW080801290526
45790CB00008B/3542